Showing and Ringcraft Explained

A Horseman's Handbook

Edited by Anne Alcock

Showing and Ringcraft Explained

Contributions by
Carol Green, Marie Stokes, Valerie Millwood,
Deirdre Robinson, Marylian Watney and
Alison Sherred

Ward Lock Limited · London

Horseman's Handbooks

TRAINING EXPLAINED
JUMPING EXPLAINED
STABLE MANAGEMENT EXPLAINED
DRESSAGE EXPLAINED
EVENTING EXPLAINED
TACK EXPLAINED
MY PONY
SHOWDRIVING EXPLAINED
LONG DISTANCE RIDING EXPLAINED
HORSE AND PONY BREEDING EXPLAINED
HORSE AILMENTS EXPLAINED

© Ward Lock Limited 1978

First published in Great Britain in 1978
by Ward Lock Limited, 82 Gower Street,
London WC1E 6EQ, a Pentos Company.
Reprinted 1979, 1982

House editor Gill Upton
Text set in Times
by Wm. Hodge and Chilver, London

Printed and bound in Great Britain by
Hollen Street Press, Slough.

British Library Cataloguing in Publication Data

Showing and ringcraft explained. – (Horseman's
    handbooks).
    I. Horses – Showing 2. Ponies
    I. Green, Carol II. Series
    636.1'08'88   SF294.5
    ISBN 0-7063 - 5574 - 1
            0-7063 - 5572 - 5pbk

Contents

Acknowledgements

The publishers would like to express their grateful thanks to the following experts for writing on the topics covered in this book: Anne Alcock on the art of riding side-saddle; Carol Green on pre-show preparation, the show horse, cobs and mountain and moorland ponies; Valerie Millwood on hacks and children's riding ponies; Deirdre Robinson on the Arab; Marie Stokes on hunters; and Marylian Watney on show driving.

We are grateful to the following for kindly providing photographs for this book: John Topham, Sally Anne Thompson, Bob Langrish, The Australian News and Information Services, Marie Stokes, Marian O'Sullivan, Pony and Light Horse, Monty, and Sport and General Press Agency and R.N. Targett for the jacket photograph.

1 Horse shows and classes

Horse shows have been an integral part of country life in Great Britain since at least the late eighteenth century, when they were usually held in conjunction with agricultural shows. These still exist in most counties and include 'county' standard horse show classes, but with the increasing popularity of horses and riding, horse shows on their own are now crammed into an extended summer season, and are in addition held in the cities too.

London has the Royal at Windsor early in the season, the Royal International at Wembley in July, the Horse of the Year Show, also at Wembley, in October, and a pre-Christmas spectacle at Olympia, so the capital is well catered for. The Royal Richmond was one of five southern shows to amalgamate to form the South of England Show on a permanent site at Ardingly, Sussex. Other major shows which cover more than one county are the East of England at Peterborough, the Great Yorkshire at Harrogate, and the Bath and West at Shepton Mallet, and in Scotland the Royal Highland Show is held at Ingliston near Edinburgh. Another with a nationalist flavour is the Royal Welsh in mid-July. Usually the first major show of the season is the Newark and Nottingham Show, where new potential stars show off their paces in public for the first time.

As the name implies, the Horse of the Year Show is intended to draw together previous winners from all over the country to do battle to find which is the best of all for a particular class. To enter for Wembley, competitors have to qualify at pre-selected shows, an exception being the cob class. Once a horse has a 'ticket for Wembley' it is an exciting occasion for those concerned with the horse, and a test of skill for the trainer, to produce it in October looking as fine and fresh as it did in the summer.

Perhaps the horse show with the greatest atmosphere of all is

7

Dublin, a mecca for horse lovers, held over a week in August at Ballsbridge. With its famous Irish bank for the show-jumpers to negotiate and the auction sales held in conjunction with it, the show enjoys a reputation for producing some of the finest quality show hunters, drawing many visitors from overseas.

Most breeds of horses and ponies also have their own annual shows: the hunter show at Shrewsbury, the Ponies of Britain at Ascot, the Welsh at Builth Wells and so on. Besides these special breed shows, the majority of horse shows have classes for hunters, hacks, Arabs, cobs, riding ponies, native breed ponies and very often donkeys, too!

Dual Gold, Middleweight Hunter of the Year, at the Horse of the Year Show at Wembley. A perfect turnout; plaited mane, 'banged tail', shiny coat and oiled hoofs; his rider in silk hat, stock, swallow-tail coat, breeches, light gloves, top boots and spurs and carrying a hunting whip.

Ready for a country show, Dual Gold's rider wears a bowler, tweed hacking jacket and tie, and carries a showing cane. The horse's coat is beautifully conditioned, with a summer bloom.

The principle behind shows has remained unaltered over the centuries: to continue to improve a given type or breed. For this reason show horses should be models of their type. Without the incentive of shows, when breeders and exhibitors alike strive for perfection, standards could slacken to the detriment of the horse and of riding in general. Once a breeder or owner has won prizes and championships at leading shows he can command high prices for his animals, and in this way the future of well-bred horses and ponies is assured. It is at horse shows also that a trainer builds his reputation for producing winning performance horses and riders. A lot of transactions take place at every major event.

Similarly, small shows play an important part, for they are needed as a stepping stone towards the higher echelons, and give encouragement to those embarking on showing. Without the small show, and even 'backyard' events, such people might fall by the wayside knowing they could not compete with the established stars, and in this way potential talent would be lost.

The development of potential talent is strongly influenced by the role of local and national horse show associations. These governing and educational bodies help set standards and rules to guide exhibitors. Classes and divisions, all with their own eligibility requirements and rules, are carefully devised to separate competitors according to ability, experience, or age. The intention is to provide everyone with fair competition and to avoid a situation where one horse and rider will always win and another lose because of an unfair handicap, such as a great difference in age or experience.

In a novice class the judge will usually bear in mind the inexperience of the exhibitors either equine or human, and make some allowances for an imperfect performance, whereas in an open class a brilliant and finished performance is expected.

In 'ladies to ride' and children's classes, more emphasis will be placed on manners and suitability. Classes are held especially for younger riders; a junior rider must be under eighteen years of age. Horse and rider age is usually determined by their status on 1 January of the current year.

In Great Britain all serious exhibitors should become members of the BHS (British Horse Society, National Equestrian Centre, Kenilworth, Warwickshire, CV8 2LR). Apart from setting standards and enforcing rules, this organization sponsors educational programmes and, in giving its sanction to big events, tries to make sure that conflicts in dates do not occur.

To the casual visitor a show class may seem rather dull, and he will probably prefer the excitement of show-jumping to the show classes, with horses or ponies seemingly just following one another around the ring. But like anything else, if that visitor can acquire some understanding of what it is all about, and begin to feel himself involved, the show class can take on new, exciting dimensions. As he learns the good points to look out for and spots the little bits of ringcraft displayed by exhibitors, the pastime takes on all-embracing interest, especially once he finds the judge agreeing with his own ringside choice of winners! He will develop an 'eye' for a horse and find himself selecting four or five, then putting them in order of preference in his mind's eye, being greatly rewarded when this order tallies with the actual result.

One of the fascinations about showing is that so much depends on opinion. A given judge at a given time may differ totally from another one somewhere else, making it quite unlike a race, where the first past the post is always the winner. Although a really top-class horse is going to win at almost any show, he is not a machine and can have an off day like any other creature; one never knows when he is going to come up against an improving youngster who may topple him from his position of supremacy. One of the most important things for an exhibitor to recognize when he enters any class is that he is submitting himself to the judge's opinion and must abide by the judge's decision. It is easy to be a winner but harder to be a graceful loser!

Once you have watched some show classes from the ringside you will see that they mostly follow a similar pattern. The riders perform the various paces in one direction from a walk round through trot to canter and then gallop at a given signal from the judge or his steward, and then reverse and repeat them 'on the other hand'. At this point the judge may have the steward line the class up before the awards are announced. Depending on the class, however, the decision may not be that simple. The judge may call his favourites into the centre, watch the rest to make sure he did not miss anyone, and then excuse those he does not like. He will then ask the remaining horses to work a little longer before he finally places the winners. Often at a big show, where the classes are large and competition very stiff, it is as great a thrill to 'make the cut' as it would be to win a class at a small event.

In some classes (those for hunters, for example), the judge will ride some, or all, of the entries himself. It is at this point that a rider with a young horse might politely excuse himself from the ring if his horse is not ready for a strange rider. A judge will usually ride every horse in a class but he may at his discretion dispense with the 'no-hopers' at the end of the line. He will usually thank them and they will leave the ring before he rides the rest. This helps classes to keep to schedule and is better than having the show run hours late. In most classes where conformation is judged, the contestants will have to strip their horses after the line-up and the judge will walk around and inspect each entrant individually or have them run up past him. As they trot past he will also note the way they move, which should be straight without any winging, toeing, dishing or going wide behind.

In any class it is essential to understand that the judge's decision is based upon what he sees in the two or ten minutes that a horse is in the ring. He can take into consideration only what he sees in that class, not how good or bad the horse was in another class or show. The clever exhibitor will realize this, and from the second he enters the ring until the very moment the class is finally lined up will show himself and his horse to best advantage. All adjustments and preparation should be complete before entering so that the rider can devote all his concentration to keeping his horse ready for the judge's eye and putting on a polished performance. It is the rider's responsibility to be seen, not the judge's to find him in the crowd! Even when the line-up is called, the exhibitors should be alert and poised — so many classes have been lost at the last instant by a rider allowing his horse to rest a leg, or by his sitting sloppily.

A good exhibitor can make a mediocre horse look good, and the reverse is also true. 'Covering up' is a great part of showmanship, and the winners are often those who are best at minimizing errors and capitalizing on their strengths. If you know your horse has a fantastic trot, make sure he is in front of the judge — but if your transition to canter is a weak spot then hide away behind the other riders, taking advantage of the fact that the judge cannot take into account what he does not see. If your horse needs a swift nudge, or you need to shorten your rein, then do it behind your judge's back. You would be ill-advised, too, always to appear beside the best-moving horse in the class — better place yourself near the mediocre entries so that your own horse is a star. Generally the biggest mistake of a novice is to get caught in the crowd; an experienced rider will keep out by himself when he wants to be seen and is continually avoiding horses that are kicking or causing trouble. Ride defensively!

Showing in halter or in-hand classes is a speciality of its own. Horse and handler turnout is all-important, but the movements that must be gone through in the arena should have been rehearsed, however simple they may be. A young horse should have been introduced to crowds and strange sights and sounds as part of his training programme, in order to behave well in the ring. The way that a horse is presented can make a tremendous difference in accentuating the good and bad points of his conformation. As in all horse show divisions, the novice exhibitor should spend a good deal of time at the ringside learning by observation.

The art of ringcraft comes only with experience. Anyone can win occasionally — the goal is to be consistently at or near the top!

2 Behind the scenes

The show ring, with all its glamour and excitement, is just the tip of the iceberg. For every minute in the spotlight, hours, days and months of preparation are involved. Not only must the horse be brought into the peak of condition physically and mentally, but he must perform his required paces, or jump his course, with sparkle and style.

For all the work entailed, it is important that the aspiring exhibitor should start out with the right horse. After the initial purchase price it costs as much to own and show a bad horse as it does a good one. The feed, travel, veterinary fees, and horse show expenses will be the same whether the horse is a backyard animal or a national champion; so it is wise to start out with the best prospect you can afford, for the nicer the horse, the better the rewards should be for all your effort and expense.

It is assumed that by the time the rider is looking for a show horse he can ride at least adequately. It is also assumed that he has a good trainer. No matter how good you may be, you need someone knowledgeable on the ground to confirm what you are feeling and to point out things which could improve your overall performance. Even Olympic calibre riders depend heavily on the feedback they get from their trainers and other expert observers. In every other competitive sport a coach or trainer is the rule, and riding should be no exception.

Buying a horse

Your trainer will probably take the initiative, if you ask him to do so, in helping you locate the right horse. The usual fee is a ten per cent commission from either the buyer or the seller. If you are working with a professional whom you trust, and you should be, this is usually a fair price to pay for the expertise, time and advice which are important in finding the right match of horse and rider. Suitability is the key, and while one horse might be a superstar for one kind of rider, he could fail miserably as someone else's mount.

In looking for a show horse or pony it is necessary to know what kind of competition you intend to enter. One animal might make an excellent equitation horse but a mediocre hunter: another might excel as a gymkhana and family pony but not make it as a show pony, although some are talented and tractable enough to be both. There is often a great difference between a 'first-horse' and a 'show horse', and a common mistake is to get a horse that is too good, or has too much potential, for your current ability. A green horse and a novice rider are usually a poor combination, as neither has the experience to help the other. The horse may lose confidence or become confused and perform poorly, if at all, while the rider also will be slow to gain the experience and confidence needed to ride well. Often the green combination involves a lot of professional help, and frustration — which is both time-consuming and expensive.

A first horse should be experienced and, above all, kind. It should be willing and confident enough to jump or perform even when the rider makes mistakes. Looks are relatively unimportant but the horse must be capable of doing, at least on an intermediate level, what the rider wants to learn. A mature first horse is preferable, it could even be into its early teens — but it should be good enough to show and place at local fixtures to give its rider a chance to gain the experience he needs for successfully riding and showing a good horse. In purchasing a first horse it is important to realize that the rider will probably make quick progress, and the horse must be capable of more advanced work so that the rider does not outgrow him too quickly. It is, therefore, essential to consider future needs as well as present realities when buying a horse for showing.

The good show prospect should possess a certain sparkle and animation that will make it stand out in a crowd. This 'presence' is what adds the finishing touch to the good looks and good performance of a top horse and separates the winners from the also-rans. It can be enhanced by certain tricks of the trade, but it cannot be created.

Conformation

The horse should be sound, with no physical defects or tendencies that could be potential causes of lameness. He must have the looks or 'conformation' needed to succeed in his chosen sphere of showing — the heavier cob type of horse would be out of place in a show hack class, for example. There are nevertheless certain conformation requirements which are basic to every show horse. A quality horse should have a small head with a good, big eye. The neck should be set on good sloping shoulders and blend well into the withers. The horse should be well coupled, with a generous girth, his hocks well let down, and the quarters strong with a nicely set tail. The feet are most important, for 'no foot, no horse' is a very true saying. They should be in proportion to the size of the horse and set on to the legs by reasonably sloping pasterns. The legs should be straight, with plenty of bone in proportion to the frame of the horse. A light horse can get away with light bone so long as it is in proportion; size of bone is more important for horses with a harder working life ahead of them, such as hunters, eventers, and racehorses. When you are thinking of buying a horse, a complete and thorough examination by a reputable veterinary surgeon is essential. For an expensive animal X-rays may be advisable.

It is a pleasure to see a fine coat, rich in colour, the mane and tail fine in texture. The quality horse has small chestnuts and ergots, the overall picture being one of superiority and refinement.

Opposite An Arab champion with the classic features of the breed, the short back, level croup, high-set tail and fine head set on an elegant neck.

Overleaf top Exercising before the show is essential to ensure that the horse is warmed up and responsive to the rider.

Overleaf below If the horse has been thoroughly and regularly groomed, his coat, mane and tail will be in good condition and a polish with a stable rubber and body brush before the show should suffice.

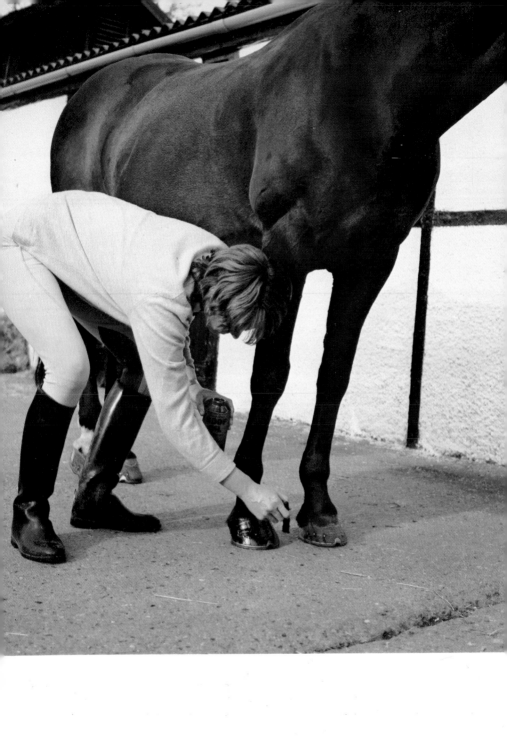

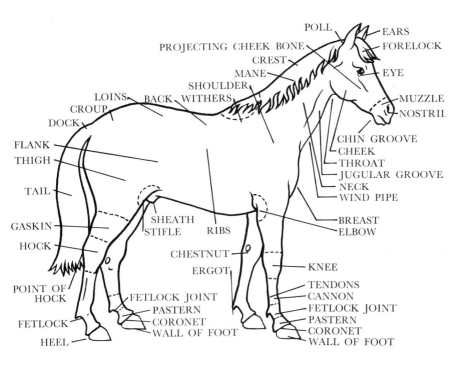

POLL
EARS
PROJECTING CHEEK BONE
FORELOCK
CREST
MANE
EYE
SHOULDER
WITHERS
MUZZLE
BACK
NOSTRIL
LOINS
CROUP
DOCK
CHIN GROOVE
CHEEK
FLANK
THROAT
THIGH
JUGULAR GROOVE
NECK
WIND PIPE
TAIL
SHEATH
GASKIN
STIFLE   RIBS
BREAST
HOCK
ELBOW
CHESTNUT
ERGOT
KNEE
POINT OF
HOCK
TENDONS
CANNON
FETLOCK JOINT
FETLOCK JOINT
PASTERN
PASTERN
FETLOCK
CORONET
CORONET
WALL OF FOOT
HEEL
WALL OF FOOT

The points of the horse.

Although the perfect horse is rarely found, the total picture should be pleasing and the animal's potential or achievements as close to your ideal as possible.

Previous page Equipment for showing, boxing and stabling should be kept clean and in good condition.

Opposite Hoof oil, painted on the hooves with a small brush will improve the appearance and condition of the feet.

Action

Action is important to every show horse, but particularly for those showing under saddle or on the flat only. Action will vary depending upon the type of horse. A show hunter or hack should move very close to the ground with a long, free stride, while a gaited horse such as the Hackney should display high knee action. All horses destined for the show ring should move straight, with the hind legs following the track of the corresponding foreleg. Except in performance classes over fences, deviations from straightness of action are usually heavily penalized. A good mover in any division should be really free in the shoulder and carry his hocks well under himself.

Stable management

To produce or keep a horse in top show condition, meticulous stable management is required. Feed, shoeing, veterinary attention, grooming and exercise or training are the five basics. They are discussed in detail in *Stable Management Explained* in this series, but a short review is in order here.

Feeding Every stable has its own feeding practices according to location and climate. Care must be taken to feed only top quality grains or mixes and to adhere to a strict schedule. A sudden change in feed, either of type or quantity, can cause severe disorders. Any change should be made gradually, and careful attention paid to the horse's condition. Some horses get too hot on a high oats ration and may fare better on some combination of grains or cubes. 'Good doers' are easy to keep and require little to maintain their energy and looks, while fussy feeders are hard. All horses should have some sort of mineral salt block and many will do well to have a vitamin or mineral supplement with their feed. Carrots, apples and turnips, which should be cut up so that there is no danger of a whole one getting stuck in the gullet, are all good and appetizing foods. Boiled barley and linseed, given two or three times a week in the evening feed, will help to keep flesh on the horse and give him a shiny coat. This is done by soaking a little barley and linseed in water in a pan overnight, bringing it to the boil the next day and simmering gently for 1½ hours until the seeds are well softened and the linseed has turned to jelly. There are three very important rules to observe whatever form of diet the horse is taking. 1) Feed little and often; four feeds a day with plenty of hay in between times helps to relieve any boredom, since this necessitates visits by you to the horse. Give your horse best quality food only. 2) Water the horse before feeding or, better still, leave fresh water always with the horse. 3) Never work a horse when he has a full stomach — horses have small stomachs compared with those of other animals of comparable size. Clean water should be available at all times, although horses should never be allowed to drink much water immediately after a feed or when they are hot from work. It is important to understand the science of feeding, as each horse is an individual, and diet is one of the most important aspects of maintaining your horse in peak condition.

Health Even the best diet is to no avail unless co-ordinated with a rigid worming programme. Depending upon location and lifestyle, most horses will need worming at least three times a year; twice is an absolute minimum. Many top show stables perform some kind of worming routine every two months. Every horse should receive tetanus vaccinations and you should consult your veterinary about inoculations against other diseases. Horses that are frequently on the road and exposed to other animals should receive whatever preventative shots are recommended. If a horse does not seem to be in as good condition as he should be, the first thing to check for is worms, the second to see if his teeth need rasping, so he can more easily chew and digest his food, and the third may be to resort to some blood tests and find out if there are any vitamin or mineral deficiencies or other disorders. Even lack of salt in a horse's diet can have a serious effect.

Shoeing A healthy horse is no use unless he is sound. One of the biggest preventative measures against lameness is frequent hoof care by a good farrier. Even a horse who is laid up for a period

Here the farrier is in the process of fitting the heated shoe to the foot.

should receive frequent attention. An unshod hoof needs to be trimmed regularly to maintain correct angles in the foot and leg and to keep the hoof itself healthy. If the hoof is allowed to grow too long the possibility of bone and tissue damage is increased, as concussion will be absorbed at a strange angle throughout the leg; an over-long hoof when shod runs the risk of corn and other foot discomforts caused by the shoe pinching. A good farrier is essential — a poor one can do more harm than good. One nail misplaced, or a foot cut too short, can cause severe lameness. An experienced farrier may be able to correct some faults in a horse's action: techniques such as rolling the toe or weighting the shoe, judiciously used, may enhance a horse's natural action. Different shoes can be useful in various types of competition: some shoes for example are designed to allow for the addition of studs to help over wet or slippery ground. As a rule, most horses will need shoeing every four to seven weeks, although this varies according to location and the time of year.

Grooming To see real results from grooming, it must be practised as a routine over an extended period. The hard work put in while shaggy winter coats abound will not really show until the horse loses the winter coat and his summer shine appears. Daily grooming not only loosens the dirt, it also massages the skin and oil

Grooming kit. *From left, top row*: water brush, tail bandage, mane and tail comb, scissors (for trimming the feathers on the heels), two sponges, hoof pick, hoof oil. *Bottom row*: body brush, metal curry comb, rubber curry comb, wisp and dandy brush.

glands. Brushing removes the dirt, a brisk massage with a hay wisp improves circulation and muscle tone, and a stable rubber or soft cloth, perhaps slightly damped, wipes away surface dust. The nose, eyes, mouth, dock and genital areas should be frequently sponged clean and it is essential to a healthy hoof that it be picked out regularly. Dry hooves may require the application of oil or grease. An important part of the grooming procedure is to keep an eye on the horse's condition and to inspect for cuts, wounds, or the development of skin conditions.

Exercise If the horse is healthy and sound, his exercise or training has a good foundation. As for the amount or type of work needed, each animal is an individual — some thrive on hard work, others get too fit to ride pleasurably, and some get bored or stale. It is up to the trainer and rider to work out a suitable programme for each animal. With a novice rider, the rider's training programme may also have to be taken into account to allow for his own progress and ability to ride and show the horse.

In general, each horse's programme must be consistent but at the same time varied. The rider must always make sure that his demands are understood; to produce a responsive, relaxed horse the signals he is asked to respond to must be consistently clear, and always enforced if not immediately obeyed. An angry or sour animal has often been created by an inefficient and inconsistent rider who constantly makes unclear or unreasonable demands on his mount. Along with a consistent programme, where the horse understands what is wanted and is never overfaced, or asked to perform tasks that are above his present level of training, an important ingredient of successful training is variety. One of the biggest challenges with a horse in the midst of a heavy show season is to keep the edge or sparkle in his performance. A routine gone through too often may be technically accurate but will lose its animation.

To keep a horse eager to work is again an individual matter. As a rule, a green horse, by the very fact of his inexperience, will find daily training more interesting than would a show veteran who thinks he knows it all. A young horse may be best brought along by short daily routines that sometimes introduce new ideas, but consistently revise, while the veteran may need only occasional schooling to sharpen him up. Almost every horse will enjoy a hack as a change of work, and while lessons can be put into practice, the more relaxed exercise will do both horse and rider good. Even a change in location can add a little interest to an old routine and help the horse to learn to keep his attention on his rider and not on new surroundings. Work up and down hills helps to build muscle and balance. More about riding and training is discussed in another volume in this series, *Training Explained.*

Pre-show training

A winning performance in the ring is marked by a sense of smoothness and presence and an apparent lack of effort. The horse should appear to perform on his own, without the rider's aid, and to slide from one pace to another with ease. Everything should be fluid and graceful. Perfection of performance can only be attained by practice, but for most horses the wise trainer will rarely put together the whole thing until the day of the show. The different movements and transitions will be rehearsed, the manoeuvres or jumps gone over and over, but the whole course or class routine will be run through only occasionally to ensure that it fits together smoothly. This way the horse does not learn to anticipate, and his interest in his work will be maintained on show day.

Rhythm is basic to any good show. An evenness and fluidity must always be present — the horse should not shorten his stride in the corners, or keep varying the height of his action. He must respond to the slightest leg and hand aids and never lose his balance in the transitions. From the moment he enters the ring until the prizes are given he must be at his best. The ideal is for your horse to look like a lion but behave like a lamb.

3 Horse show preparations

Apart from the extended and gradual conditioning and training that is the background to the show season, there is a certain amount of direct pre-show preparation that every exhibitor must go through. This will vary depending upon whether you travel alone or with a big stable and whether you are exhibiting mostly at one-day shows or at week-long events.

Early in the year a tentative show schedule can be arranged. Priorities must be established for each horse, and care taken that horse and rider should they prove successful, will not be upgraded until they are ready. It is essential to be absolutely familiar with all status and eligibility rules of your governing associations so that you do not, inadvertently, move your horse into a new division until he is ready. Sometimes a horse's career must be planned several years in advance.

Once you have planned what shows you will compete in, you must ensure that your training schedule will produce your horse at the correct level of performance. The horse must never be over-faced, particularly not in the show ring, and should always be completely competent at home before he is asked to perform at a show. If, as is the case in many classes, he may be ridden by the judge, he should be used to performing for strangers.

It is a great advantage for a young horse to attend a couple of shows as a spectator only, to allow him to become familiar with the whole show atmosphere. Only when he is relaxed in strange surroundings will he be able to perform his best. At his first few shows as an exhibitor he should be entered in the simplest classes only — and three a day is usually enough for a baby. The aim is to make showing an enjoyable, not frightening or tiring, experience.

Once your show schedule has been decided upon it is necessary to send your entries in by the deadlines. Late entries may be accepted at an additional fee, or in some cases rejected altogether. If the show is at some distance from your home it may be necessary to make overnight accommodation arrangements for both you and your horse well in advance.

In Britain the painkiller (phenylbutazone or butazolydin) 'bute' is illegal for showing though permitted for show-jumping and eventing. This is a controversial point as while it is useful under veterinary supervision, in relieving temporary soreness (a bruise, for example) it could also allow an animal who is genuinely injured, and should be resting, to work and perhaps be caused further damage. It could also mask some hereditary unsoundness, which is another reason why its use is banned in showing.

If you will be stabling your horse overnight at a show be sure that bedding is provided — if not, you will have to plan to take your own. Often, the first night's bedding is provided but you must purchase or bring with you the extra needed for a four or five-day stay. Stables may not have latches, so plan to bring your own locks and, of course, you should count on bringing your own water buckets and feed tubs. Do not forget mucking-out tools and, if you are renting an additional stall as a tack room, your portable saddle racks and other fittings. You will also need the full grooming kit, first-aid box for you and your horse, head-collar and rope, and summer sheet and anti-sweat rug for the horse after the show. A tack-cleaning hook is always useful, as are conveniences like a lamp, an electric water heater, and a coffee pot if electricity is available. A torch is always handy. Many big stables fit out their tack rooms in a decor worthy of a living room, and it provides a comfortable retreat or headquarters while at the show — often doubling up as the night watchman or groom's bedroom! If you are travelling with a stable, most of the horse's accommodation and travel arrangements will be handled by your trainer. It is wisest to bring the feed your horse is used to unless you are certain you can purchase it at the show. As a word of warning: never let your horse drink out of a common water trough, as it is an invitation to disease.

During the show season your car boot will become your travelling tack room. Equip it well! Along with all your many regular requirements you will want to carry spares in case of loss or breakage. Extra buckles, lead ropes and reins are never regretted. It is a good idea to keep a checklist in your boot lid so as not to forget an important item. Basic tools like a hammer and nails can be indispensable.

Travelling

If you are hauling your own trailer or driving your own box or truck it is a heavy responsibility to make certain that all brakes, lights, locks, suspensions, hitches and other details are in excellent repair. The horse should be well protected for travelling with a tail bandage, tailguard, knee pads, stable bandages and perhaps a poll guard. The poll guard, made of foam rubber, is sewn on to the headcollar and protects the horse's head from damage if he should become excited in the trailer. If the horse is to wear any special equipment on a trip, make sure that he first becomes accustomed to it in his own stable. A disadvantage of some travelling gear is that it can be uncomfortably warm on a hot day. The business of loading a young horse should not be left until the day he has to be transported to a show; he should be used to short trips and load-

Putting on a tail bandage; take care not to drop the tail bandage, and keep the end in your hand.	The end of the tail bandage is folded over when the tail bandage has gone round the tail once.	The finished tail bandage. It should be neat, and not tight enough to restrict circulation.

30

Travelling boots are a useful alternative to the stable bandage, to protect the legs while travelling.

ing and unloading before he is ever taken in a van to a horse show. It is as much a part of his training as any other exercise and it should be well-rehearsed on his home-ground beforehand. Make the whole experience of loading as pleasant as possible for the young horse: position the trailer in such a way to get maximum light inside, open all windows and ventilators for light and air and reward your horse, once inside the trailer, with a small feed. Always walk the horse slowly and calmly to the trailer, without rushing him, and remain close to his shoulder until he is safely in the trailer. In this way the horse will have no reason to fear loading or travelling.

Turnout for showing

The turnout of horse and rider in the show ring is all-important. 'Handsome is as handsome does' is true, but first impressions are lasting and a judge cannot help but be heavily influenced by appearances, for that is certainly part of the game. Fortunately at small shows and novice events, neatness and cleanliness is the rule, but as you and your horse progress, a custom fit is essential. Often, by careful shopping, a subtle but striking outfit can be arranged economically, especially if good second-hand equipment is available, but it is sometimes necessary to go to considerable expense to acquire the right equipment. Fit is the prime concern for comfort as well as looks. In general it is better to stay conservative in colour choice. Before embarking on a spending spree, become thoroughly familiar with the options and requirements of your show divisions.

The one item that should never be scrimped upon is your saddle. It is worth going overboard on this purchase to get exactly the right fit for both you and your horse, as a good saddle can enhance performance considerably and a bad one really hinder it. The horse must be absolutely comfortable to perform his best.

It goes without saying that you, your horse and all your equipment and tack should be meticulously presented. Tack will need to be wiped over after every class and all metal parts should be polished and shining.

Assuming that a faithful grooming routine has been practised regularly, pre-show or pre-class grooming presents no problem. The horse's clean coat should be wiped over with a towel to remove any dust. Feet should be oiled or blackened depending upon the current fashion. If there are flies about, it is essential to use an insect repellent, as no horse looks its best when fidgeting and tossing because of pests. You may want to spray a sheen on the coat or put a little vaseline or baby oil around the eyes. Hair conditioner can help the tail and whitener can brighten your horse's socks, should he have any. The mane and tail should be plaited, combed, or fixed according to the type of class, and as close to your class as possible to ensure that they are as neat and impressive-looking as can be. A clever plaiting job can make a short neck look longer by using many miniature plaits, and a well-shaped tail can accentuate or improve the hindquarters. If you do give your horse a shampoo bath, it should be done infrequently and never too close to show day as it will remove the oils and shine from the coat. A pure water rinse is usually sufficient, and does not remove the oils.

The finishing touch to a nice turnout of horse and rider is good trimming. Again, this is an art, and like plaiting, should be practised long in advance of the show season. The usual procedure (though not in all types of class — e.g. breed classes) is to trim excess hair from the muzzle, under the head, eyes, ears, poll, fetlocks, pastern, and coronet areas. A good job will be invisible: it accentuates a fine horse's features and can minimize the coarseness of a heavier animal.

Before the rider actually shows the horse he should be thoroughly familiar with ring procedure, having observed many other classes before first competing himself. As you are only in the ring for a short period it is essential to allow yourself plenty of time to get turned out and warmed up. Many classes have been lost because an exhibitor did not allow himself enough time to prepare adequately. After the class the horse should be thoroughly cared for, and at the end of a hard day a liniment wash-down can be a welcome relief for tired muscles.

This behind-the-scenes part of showing is half the fun of it — no one is a consistent winner without faithful homework and preparation!

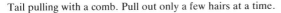
Tail pulling with a comb. Pull out only a few hairs at a time.

4 Show hunters

More a type than a breed, the hunter is a result of selective breeding, something that has been greatly encouraged by the Hunters' Improvement Society. This admirable scheme selects Thoroughbred stallions it considers suitable for breeding hunters – good bone, conformation, temperament, soundness, stamina and so on – and issues them with a premium. They then stand at stud in every county throughout Britain so that everyone has an opportunity of taking advantage of the scheme which is at a reduced price for members. An annual stallion show is held when premiums are issued, and breeders will naturally be pleased if they obtain a nomination for their mare to the champion stallion.

The ideal hunter looks a picture and will win in the show ring but his performance, ability and soundness are, above all, what matter most for the hunting field. Ideally he will have a good-looking head, wide-set, large, honest-looking eyes, a slightly arched neck, good sloping shoulders, short cannon bones (which must not be spindly if he is to carry you through deep and rough ground out hunting), ample 'jumping' quarters, and good hocks which propel him over obstacles and through mud.

Show hunters

The hunter's weight-carrying capacity can be assessed by his size, the strength and substance of limbs, loins, back, hocks and knee joints. Well-shaped, matching feet are essential. He must not be 'tied in at the knee' or over-topped – that is, with too heavy a body for his legs. He must be in good proportion, generous in character, bold and tireless. He will often be a pure Thoroughbred, and nearly always at least part-bred.

The ladies' hunter must have all the above qualities, and in

A show hunter cantering for the judges, going nicely. The rider is holding his showing cane with his hand too low down it, and could risk a jab if the unexpected happens.

addition superb manners, especially if he is ridden side-saddle. Under the Hunters' Improvement Society rules there are five categories of show hunters, and classes are held for them at leading shows up and down the country. They are: small hunter, for mares or geldings over 14.2 hands and not over 15.2 hands; lightweight hunter, capable of carrying up to 13 stone (82.5kg.); middleweight hunter up to 14 stone (99kg.); heavyweight hunter, over 14 stone (99kg.); and ladies' hunter, suitable for and to be ridden by a lady. This last class can be sub-divided into riding astride or side-saddle.

35

In addition there is a novice hunter class in which any of the above can compete if they have not won a first prize value £15 at home or abroad in ridden hunter, hack or cob classes. It is a good class for a young horse to gain experience.

Working hunters

In addition to the show classes there are working hunter classes, usually divided between large (over 15.2 hands) and small (under 15.2 hands) hunters. Blemishes are acceptable up to a point, and the horse's looks can be more 'workmanlike', with an abundance of bone, for in this class competitors are required to jump.

The HIS has a scale of marks for the sections divided into jumping, ride and conformation. The jumping course should be judged as a whole, as if the rider were out hunting, and should be jumped at a fair hunting pace. The show-jumper could come in, jump slowly and precisely, perhaps propping into a fence but then cat-jumping clear over it, whereas a genuine hunter type going smoothly may brush the top of the fence and dislodge it. If that happened out hunting, the fence would be fixed and would not come down, so in this way a judge may not penalize a knock too severely. On the other hand, if a horse hit a fence low down and hard, that would cause certain grief in the hunting field and must be penalized. Refusals are penalized by 10 penalties for the first, 20 for the second and elimination for the third, which is as it should be, for no one wants a 'stopper' out hunting.

Thus the horse who 'rolls' off a pole may, if his quality, action, presence and ride are good, still win a class. Jumping should not account for more than forty per cent of the total marks, or working hunter classes could degenerate into jumping classes with sub-show standard horses taking part. It is basically a practical showing

Opposite Washing the horse's tail with a bucket of warm water, a large sponge and special shampoo.

Overleaf The tail should be carefully rinsed in a bucket of clean warm water.

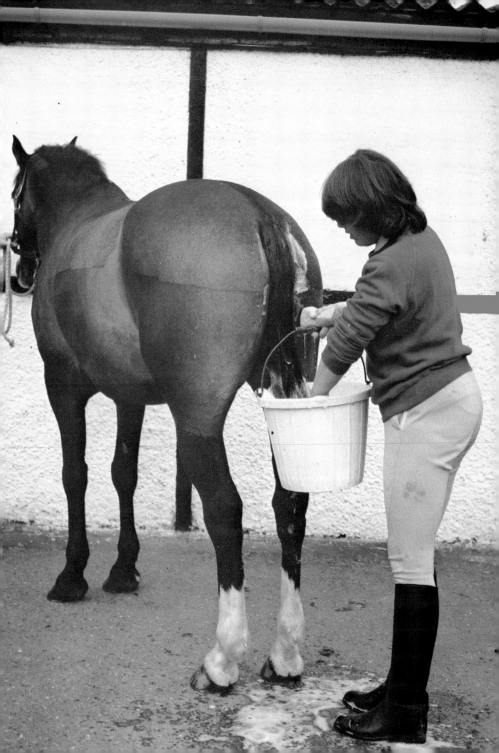

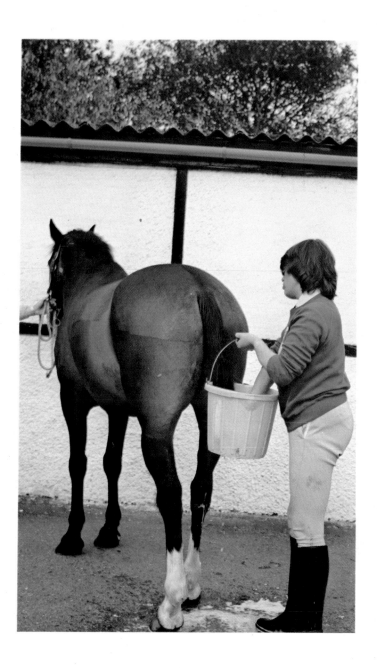

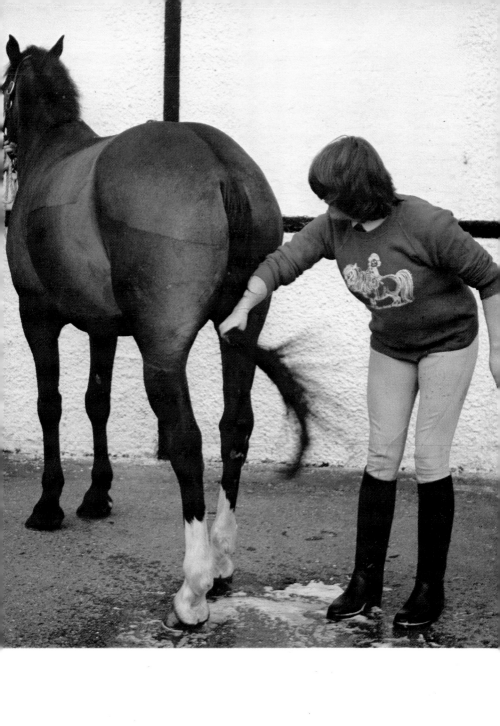

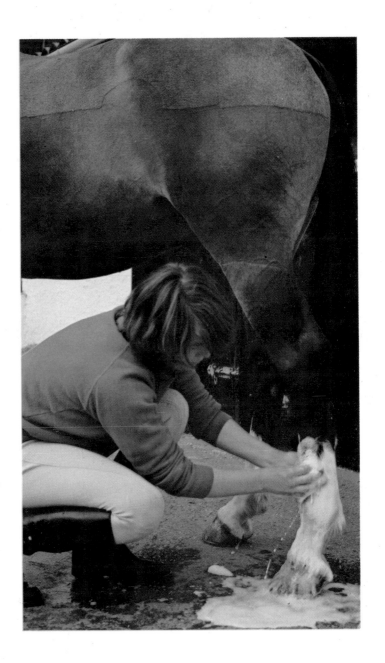

Working Hunter Class for Children under 14 at the Leicester City Show. The jumping phase; this pony has his legs well tucked under him as he clears the rustic fence with room to spare. Pony and rider are well co-ordinated.

class, where perhaps more horse and not so much refinement is called for. There will be about six rustic, hunting-type fences, usually about 3ft 9in (1.15m) high and the course will involve changes of direction to test obedience and smoothness. Usually the working hunters jump first and then proceed as in an ordinary showing class.

Previous page The tail is dried by shaking and flicking it to remove the surplus water.

Opposite Washing the horse's white socks will enhance his appearance for the show ring.

The hunter should not get over-excited and should have long strides that cover the ground effortlessly. In preparing for a show, his daily schooling programme must consist of plenty of slow work up and down hills to improve his balance and the use of his shoulders. Avoid hard ground or too much road work, as this could cause the horse unnecessary jarring and concussion to the foot and lower limbs, with resulting windgalls, splints, curbs or spavins. Windgalls are puffiness around the joints and are usually temporary, disappearing once the horse works on soft ground, but the other complaints are permanent bony growths that will ruin a horse's show prospects. You have to be particularly careful not to overwork a young horse on hard ground before its bones have hardened up sufficiently. If a splint forms on a tendon it can cause permanent lameness, perhaps necessitating an operation to have it 'fired off'. The horse can then lead a normal life in any field except showing. In the ring the horse must be happy to be ridden on a long rein in walk, trot and canter, and return to walk and trot without effort, all the while showing good manners. The working hunter must be taught to jump freely in a galloping stride.

Hunters in hand

Most larger shows have classes for young hunters shown in hand. The judge will be looking for stock he considers likely to develop into a hunter, but there are no weight categories. This results in the best-grown youngster usually winning although if a smaller or lighter animal shows more class and is better put together, it will be put up. There are usually classes for a brood mare in foal or who has had a foal that year, for her foal, then for yearlings, two-year-olds and three-year-olds. It is the first and second horses from these last three classes which usually compete to see which is the champion hunter in hand.

The in-hand hunter should be just as meticulously turned out as a ridden hunter, with a glossy coat and plaited mane. His tail can be plaited too, to show off his quarter. He would be shown in a bridle and lead rein, and his handler — also neatly turned out — should carry a cane. A male handler can wear a bowler hat, hacking jacket and tie, and slacks, while a woman can wear a hat or scarf instead of a bowler.

Young hunters in professional hands are often kept in the stable all summer, corn fed and with a light rug on at night to keep the coat down. The result is a blooming, well-grown horse, but one that may well be too fat. Although he is likely to do exceptionally well in hand, the over-fat horse may have difficulty doing well once he is broken and ridden. Energy-giving, fattening foods without sufficient exercise are stored as glycogen in the muscles, and when this is broken down lactic acid is released, which can cause permanent muscle and kidney damage.

5 Hacks

One of the true British classes, which carries on the elegance and tradition of a more leisurely age in showing, is the hack class. The show hack could really be described as the actor of showing: besides possessing excellent conformation and being well trained, it must have presence and personality and be graceful in movement.

A hack must be a quality horse, whether Thoroughbred, part-bred or Anglo-Arab, so that with a well-turned-out rider, it conjures up a true picture of elegance.

Today a hack is a pleasure horse, and as such should be a beautiful ride and schooled to the standard of novice dressage. For a show, however, you want a freer, lighter movement than in a dressage test, as an important part of the hack class is the minute or so of individual display given by each competitor. In this time the horse must show the paces of walk and trot, canter a figure of eight and produce extended canter, halt and canter. To do this effectively, the rider must also be competent and polished.

If you are new to showing hacks, the first thing to do is to join the British Show Hack and Cob Association. This association lays down the rules for all affiliated hack classes. The address is: The British Show Hack and Cob Association, National Equestrian Centre, Kenilworth, Warwickshire CV8 2LR.

Hack classes

The hack classes recommended by the Association are:

Novice hack A novice is a hack which has not won a total of £25 or more in hack classes, ladies' and pair classes excepted, at shows affiliated to the Association, at the closing date of entry of the show concerned.

44

Breeding and sensible nature show in the calm gaze of this hack. He wears an ornamental browband and his mane neatly brushed to one side.

Hacks Mares or geldings exceeding 14.2 hands and not exceeding 15 hands.

Hacks Mares or geldings exceeding 15 hands and not exceeding 15.3 hands.

Ladies' hacks Mares or geldings exceeding 14.2 hands and not exceeding 15.3 hands, suitable to carry and to be ridden by a lady side-saddle.

All these classes are similar in procedure to other showing classes except for the individual show, and a change of leg at the canter is always required instead of galloping. It is judged in three parts: the performance — the horse ridden round in the class at walk, trot, canter and change of leg, then the individual display; the ride it gives the judge; conformation and movement in hand.

Hack conformation

Quality, movement and presence are the most important characteristics for the hack. For his movement, he must go off his hocks but must not exaggerate his knee in the way of a Hackney. He

Standing quietly but alert, this hack's nice head suggests a kindly temperament. His shiny coat indicates hours of grooming, and his good quarters are emphasized by the 'quartering' pattern on his rump.

must use his shoulders, and this will be helped if he has room between his elbow and ribs. If he is 'tied in at the elbow' his movements may be contracted, making it impossible for him to throw out his toe in extension.

Quality will include a small, intelligent, Thoroughbred or Arab-type head, well placed on to the neck, which should join sloping shoulders and a good wither. His front should be excellent, but when looking for a horse with a good length of rein, be on your guard against a short neck on a good shoulder or a long neck on upright shoulders, both of which give a false impression of length of rein. Often it is not until you are on top of such horses that you notice these faults, because they are not noticeable from the ground

The show hack wants to be 'well ribbed up', with no hollow between the last rib and the point of hip. The hocks should not stand away from the horse behind, or he will be hard to balance and will finish by going on his forehand.

If two hacks in a class have all the desirable qualities of straight action, perfect manners, and no blemishes or faults in conformation, it will be the one whose personality shines through best that will be likely to win. The indefinable quality of 'presence' and pride is essential if you want your hack to succeed. It is a gift that care in training and conditioning may emphasize, but cannot produce unless the horse is born with it. Experience with horses, and a careful study of other competitors, will train your eye to identify this presence and eventually to ensure that any horse you buy, however green he may be, possesses it.

Look out for blemishes and signs of weak limbs, especially if the horse has come out of racing. It may not have been able to stand the going, but a show horse must have good feet and limbs as it is often working on hard ground throughout the summer. Apart from the judging aspect, good feet and strong (as opposed to thick) limbs are necessary or the horse may pull out lame on the day of an important show. The basic facts of conformation apply, whatever you are going to use a horse for, and a badly put together animal will give a bad ride. It is impossible to train a badly made horse to a high degree: he will never achieve the perfect balance which is so important to a show hack.

A champion hack, ridden side-saddle. An ideal hack has a long back and a low stride, which gives a more comfortable ride side-saddle, particularly at the trot, when the rider does not rise, and so requires an animal which moves as smoothly as possible.

Turnout

When showing your hack, your turnout must be perfect, your horse beautifully groomed and plaited with well-fitting, spotless tack. You too should be properly dressed, with a well-fitting hacking jacket being quite in order, with cap or bowler, for a country show. Save the dressing up with stocks and silk hats for the big shows, such as Wembley.

The judging is the same for small and large hack classes but you get slightly different types in each. The small hack is often a part-bred Arab or of pony breeding, although it should look not like a pony, but more a small horse. The large hack is all horse, often Thoroughbred, but not a riding' horse', which has a class of its own, and is also run under the rules of the British Show Hack and Cob Association.

The 'riding horse' class is for the horse with quality and substance, which should be as well trained as a hack but capable of galloping on and jumping if required. A riding horse should be a more general-purpose animal than a hack: it should be suitable for hunting, riding-club activities and so on. It is judged in the same way as hacks, the emphasis being on training, and may also be required to give an individual show. A riding horse should be more strongly built than a hack, but still full of quality and presence. It should also be ridden on more strongly than a hack, and should be a balanced, easy, enjoyable ride for the judge, even though the hack's degree of refinement is not required of it.

6 Cobs

One of the nicest old-fashioned sights in the show ring today is the class for the heavyweight cob. In spite of his solid appearance, a good show cob springs over the ground belying the weight of his body. His primary purpose is to carry elderly, heavy riders and as such he must be 'as safe as houses' with immaculate manners. Being fairly close to the ground – a show cob must not stand more than 15.1 hands – it is easier for an elderly person to mount him and, having very little or no Thoroughbred blood in him, he should be quiet and calm. However, if he is to receive only limited assistance from the saddle, he must be well enough trained to go at whatever may be the required pace, and to stop easily the moment he is asked. The cob makes an excellent hunter through heavy wooded country where there are low boughs, deep mud and timber to negotiate. He has exceptionally strong cannon bones, great depth of girth and heart room and a short back, all of which helps in such country. Until it was made illegal, all cobs had docked tails and they are usually hog-maned. Cobs are less popular than they used to be; when there were many more of them about there were often two classes for them, lightweight and heavyweight, but now there is just the one class, for cobs not exceeding 15.1 hands and capable of carrying more than 14 stone (99kg). A nice cob can be a good gymkhana and family horse.

Training

It is best to start training the young horse in a school or manège by working on a single track, then changing the rein by turning down the centre and going to the opposite track, riding loops, circles, voltes, turn on the forehand, demi-pirouettes, serpentines and changes of direction within the circle. All these movements

Cromwell, the Champion Cob at Hickstead in 1976. Solid and rounded in shape, with a deep girth and strong quarters, the arched and elegant neck of this cob gives him great charm.

should be practised first at the walk. When the horse has mastered these basic movements at the walk, you should progress through to trot and ride the movements at the faster paces. Very often the cob tends to lose impulsion on the turns and this should be anticipated: ride him energetically and firmly forward, so that both rhythm and impulsion are maintained.

By working the cob on turns, circles, and transitions you will begin to improve his suppleness, athletic ability, and balance. Good balance is very important for two reasons: first, he will give you a much safer and more enjoyable ride; second, the horse will be more comfortable and will not overtax any one leg. From the normal balanced state one must go on to develop what is called fluid balance; this is the shifting of the horse's point of balance smoothly forward and back without jolting the horse and rider. It is particularly important that the cob is taught to go freely

Comfortable and as safe as houses, but with a sparkle of gaiety, this cob has all these qualities as he canters in the ring at the Royal Windsor Show. A well-schooled cob should be totally reliable, with a responsive animation for an enjoyable ride.

forward from the lightest possible aid, performing smoothly without loss of balance. By his very shortness and conformation, the badly-trained cob becomes a dull, stuffy, jolting ride. The well-trained cob, on the other hand, is workmanlike, carrying himself with dignity, complete obedience, and moving with well-balanced and comfortable strides. In short, we are looking for good free movement with the horse working calmly, obediently and actively.

In the ring

The judge will wish to see the cob work at all paces. At the walk he will be looking for strength, a walk that is forward-going, safe and unhurried — as befitting an elderly gentleman's ride. At the trot his manners must be perfect. The cob should move with little or no knee action and he must be able to lengthen and shorten his stride at the trot, again showing good manners and reliability. At the canter the judge will wish to see the horse cover the ground with effortless strides, and he must be well balanced and controlled. The cob is not usually asked to gallop, although some judges do include it — naturally they will not expect to see the horse cover the ground as effortlessly as the hunter. From the canter the cob must return to trot calmly and quietly without resistance. Depending on how many horses are in the class, the rider may be asked to give an individual show. This gives the judge an opportunity to see the horse move by itself on both reins at walk, trot and canter, and to take in the overall picture. He will expect the horse to stand motionless when mounted, to have easy paces which are a pleasure to sit to, and to give a willing and responsible ride without becoming excited. The reverse situation is also undesirable; a cob which is lazy and gives a sloppy, boring ride. When he is trotted up in hand for the individual scrutiny of the judge he must have straight action.

A good cob cannot fail to catch your eye. Indeed, they are horses of great appeal, calm, dignified, and with plenty of character.

7 Mountain and moorland ponies

Indigenous to nine separate areas of the British Isles since time immemorial are the wonderfully sturdy, hardy native ponies. In spite of modern mechanization and development, they have retained their homelands and their contrasting characteristics. Many are now reared in the luxury of studs and are crossed with Arab and Thoroughbred blood to make top-class show ponies and performers, but the native pony itself is encouraged by classes for it at most leading shows, thereby preserving one of Britain's most ancient heritages.

The native ponies range in size from the diminutive Shetlands in those far northern islands to another Scot, the Highland, which reaches 14.2 hands. The south of England has the New Forest, Dartmoor and Exmoor breeds, while the Welsh Mountain is an attractive part of the hillside scenery in the Principality. Ireland boasts the rugged Connemara, and in the north of England the Pennine Chain divides the Fell of Cumberland and Westmorland now Cumbria to the west, from the Dale of Northumberland to the east.

The Shetland pony

The Shetland is one of the best known and most popular of ponies, with its appealing, 'toy-dog' looks, a cuddly woolly coat and impish expression and personality. He thrives on the hardest of conditions, enduring snow, ice and almost non-existent fodder and shelter. The harshness of the Shetland winters sometimes drives him onto the beaches with only seaweed to eat, yet his coat shines – indeed, seaweed extract is used as a conditioner for racehorses! He is so small that he is usually measured in inches instead of hands, standing from a mere 26in (64.8cm) to the stud book

The Shetland pony's diminutive size and abundant mane and tail make him suited to the harsh winds and driving sleet and rain of his original homeland. The mane and tail are pulled very little or not at all, and are brushed out to their natural length, and the feather is left on the fetlocks.

Shetland ponies; tiny and very strong, here displaying characteristic stubbornness, which makes pure Shetlands not totally suitable for first ponies; they need a good deal of work. But they are hardy and versatile and very game little ponies.

limit of 42in (106.7cm), and he retains his smallness even when bred on warmer, lusher pastures. Ponies have probably lived on the Shetlands since the Bronze Age, some 2500 years ago. Before there were any roads in his homeland he was almost the main means of transport, ideal because of his sure-footedness. His size brought him a much less pleasant job in the nineteenth century, when he was in great demand for underground work in the mines. Shetlands are now used mainly for children's first ponies and pets, although they are also excellent in harness, so that their popularity has spread across the world.

The Welsh Mountain

The mountains and deep, green valleys of Wales have produced one of the most beautiful — and ancient — ponies of the world, the Welsh Mountain. Pretty, intelligent, agile and sound, the Welsh

Arab breeding shows in the head of this Welsh Mountain stallion (Section A), in his slightly flared nostrils, large dark eyes and dark markings around his eyes and muzzle. His head is well set-on to his powerful beautifully arched neck, and shows pride and courage. This breed produces very useful results when crossed with a larger quality horse.

Opposite Legs should be carefully rinsed and dried, particularly the heels, to prevent soreness and cracking.

Overleaf top When fitting a stable or travelling bandage, the gamgee, used to give extra protection against knocking in a box or stable, is put on under the bandage.

Overleaf below The bandage is applied with the end sticking up, on the second turn the end is folded down, to prevent it slipping.

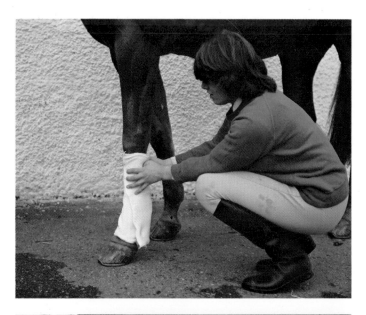

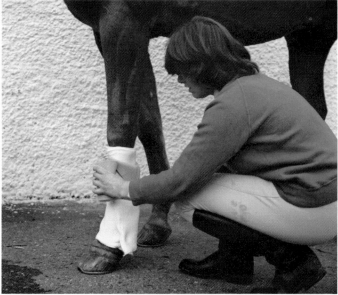

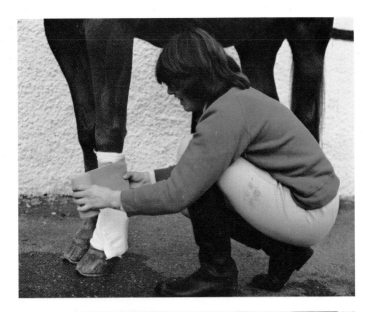

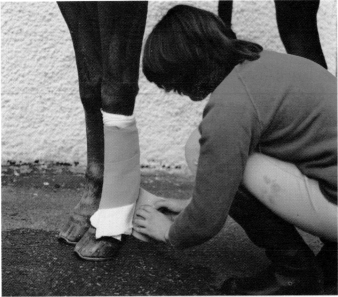

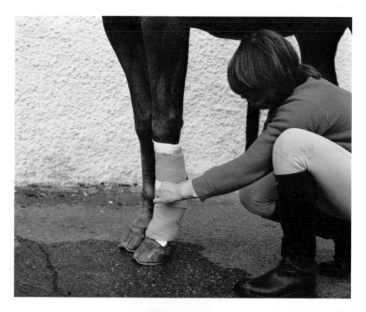

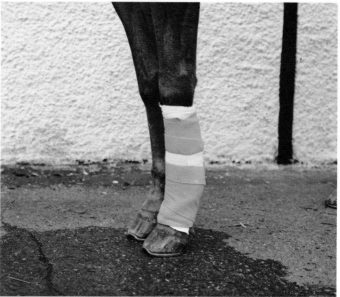

In perfect summer condition, this Welsh Cob (Section D) has a powerful, compact body, strong neck, sturdiness and keenness, which suggest a bouncing, tireless action.

Mountain has an Arab-like quality to his head with slightly dished face, small, prick ears and bold eyes. Gentle, yet courageous, with good movement and an aptitude for jumping, the Welsh make excellent children's ponies, well suited to showing. In Wales they are still used for shepherding, hunting and perhaps taking the farmer to market.

Previous page (top) As the bandage is put on, each turn round the leg should be even.

Previous page (below) It is important that the bandage is taken right into the heels so that there is less risk of the horse injuring himself.

Opposite top The bandage is taken over the heels and brought evenly up the leg and secured by Velcro fastening.

Opposite below The finished bandage will give warmth and protection to the leg.

A fine New Forest pony in his natural surroundings. With his small feet and good riding shoulder, this pony is a good example of his breed. This one has an attractive strongly arched neck and his head shows keenness.

The New Forest

When the forest covering much of Hampshire was declared a Royal Hunting Forest some 900 years ago, it became known as the New Forest. The pony by that name which breeds and roams there makes a good riding pony even for a small adult, standing from about 12.2 to 14.2 hands. Accustomed to tourists' cars driving through the forest, he is nearly always good in traffic, an incalculable advantage these days, although sadly some are killed by cars every year. He is friendly, and easy to break and train. Only registered stallions are allowed to run in the Forest, about 150 of them mingling with some 2,000 mares, mostly brown in colour. The stallions are rounded up and inspected each spring and any that do not meet a specific standard are rejected, in order to maintain a high standard of pony breed.

Exmoor and Dartmoor ponies

The Exmoor is considerably smaller than the New Forest, rarely exceeding 12.2 hands, but he is strongly built and up to more weight than his size suggests, happily carrying adults across the moor for a day's hunting. The distinctive feature of the Exmoor is his mealy muzzle; the same oatmeal-colour markings are often around his eyes, under his belly and inside his ears and legs, too. Seen from the front, his eyes should look prominent and wide, rather like frog's eyes, but kindly. Predominantly bay or brown, the true Exmoor has no white markings. His ears and nostrils are also wide-set and he has a thick, sturdy body. Life on Exmoor has made him sure-footed and, as such, a great friend to farmers who roam the moor looking after their livestock.

An Exmoor pony mare and foal, with the characteristic mealy muzzles of their breed, and rather prominent, kindly eyes. A mare and foal should be led separately in the show ring, the foal behind.

A very pretty Dartmoor pony filly, a champion at the Royal Show at Stoneleigh, Warwickshire. She has a small elegant head, nicely carried, slender, dainty legs and a glistening coat. Her long tail is a typical feature. Dartmoor ponies stand up to very hard winters on the moors, and food has to be dropped to them by helicopter when they are stranded by snow and unable to get to villages to be fed.

On neighbouring Dartmoor, bleaker than Exmoor, the native Dartmoor pony stands about 12.2 hands and, with his good head carriage and 'plenty in front' is an ideal child's first pony. He also makes a good foundation for cross-breeding to produce a larger, child's second pony. Roaming the windswept moor, dotted by towering granite tors, this native pony is also sure-footed and very hardy.

Fell and Dales ponies

Two larger, utility-type ponies, the Dales and the Fell, have served the people of the north of England since earliest times. The Fell pony of the Lake District is black, dark brown or dark bay with an occasional grey, with a full, rather curly mane and tail and well-

A Fell pony in good summer condition, with a magnificent coat. His longish back and short strong legs are usual features of this breed, as are his curly full tail and the feather on his fetlocks, left on, as for all mountain and moorland breeds, when shown as such in hand.

feathered heels, and it has been improved by selective breeding since about 1900. The height limit is 14 hands, and his legs are exceptionally strong and sound. High head carriage, sloping shoulders, deep girth and prominent action make him a striking pony. Besides being used for shepherding, pulling a trap to market, working on the land and riding, he was, in times gone by, also used in trotting races. Another occupation was as a pack-pony, pulling lead from the mines to the ships at Newcastle, his strength has always served him well.

Closely akin to the Fell is the Dales pony, noted for his long mane and tail and profuse amount of feather on his heels. He is also a dark colour and, as one of the largest of the native ponies with strength and bone to match, he can carry a 16-stone (102kg) man or pull a ton (1016kg) of weight. He was also a great favourite for trotting races and earned his living on the farm or pulling a

A Dales pony stallion, his spirit showing as he rolls his eye, showing the white. His dark colour and profuse feather are typical. His strength and spanking action at the trot made him popular in harness and for trotting races. This pony is an excellent example.

trades man's cart. When motor vehicles took over, many Dales were slaughtered for meat — to such an extent that their future was threatened. Luckily, a few dedicated breeders remained. Then, in the 1950's when trekking became fashionable, a new, perfectly acceptable role became available to them. They are ideal for this job, where the riders are mostly novices, because Dales are quiet to handle, sure-footed and tough. Now there is an active breed society and with the Dale's popularity for riding and in harness his future looks assured.

The Highland

The strongest of all the native ponies is the Highland, with stallions having up to as much as 10in (25cm) of bone. Their colour is often dun with a black dorsal stripe. They have soft, flowing manes and tails, finely arched necks, compact bodies and good heads with wide-apart expressive eyes and neat little ears. Mostly found on the farms in Scotland, the Highland probably originated from Northern Europe, although he now has some Arab blood in him. Stocky and strong, the Highland is also intelligent and once he has made friends with a person he is always willing to please unless soured by rough or unkind handling.

The strength of this Highland pony is expressed by his powerful neck and deep body; his ancestors carried heavy loads, such as dead stags, over steep and wild country, so he is very tough and sure-footed, and well able to endure adverse weather conditions.

Highland pony with a magnificent mane and forelock, brushed out to their natural length. His muzzle whiskers are left on, not trimmed, and this adds to his kindly, good-natured expression.

The Connemara

Although not strictly part of Great Britain, the ninth native pony is the Connemara, from that lovely, rugged, wild stretch of Western Ireland. This is a particularly popular pony with children as he makes an excellent hunter and jumper and is good looking enough to show in working hunter pony classes. At up to 14 hands, he makes an ideal second pony and has a superb temperament. When crossed with a Thoroughbred, the Connemara can make a top-class

Connemara pony at the Ponies of Britain Show at Ascot. The only native Irish breed, it is very popular for cross-breeding with Thoroughbreds, to combine quality with hardiness. This pony is in magnificent condition, with a lovely coat, mane and tail, and has superb conformation.

competition horse. The Irish guard the breed likeness by holding inspections of the wild ponies in Connemara every year, accepting only those ponies which are true to type and licensing all the stallions.

Breed societies

Before native ponies may be shown they must be registered with their respective breed societies: Dales Pony Society, Dartmoor Pony Society, Exmoor Pony Society, Fell Pony Society, Highland Pony Society with the Shetland Pony Stud Book Society, New Forest Pony Society, and Welsh Pony and Cob Society. Details of these societies' activities and addresses may be obtained from the National Equestrian Centre, Kenilworth, Warwickshire CV8 2LR.

Showing in hand

In-hand pony classes may be for foals, yearlings, two and three-year-olds, so read the schedule carefully and be sure to enter your horse in the right class. Training for the show ring should begin from the earliest possible age, ideally with the foal. This is discussed at length in *Training Explained.*

The art of showing in hand is to present your youngster to the best advantage, and the only way to learn is to stand at the ringside at the big show and watch the experts. Then what you learn must be practised at home to perfection. Train your youngster in a show headcollar and white lead rein (not a chain), using the bit only when necessary, and practise trotting the pony in a straight line. This will help the judge to see your pony's best points, and you will gain marks for its obedience and free, straight action.

Foals may be shown in their slip (that is, a small leather headcollar specially designed for foals with a cross-strap adjustment at the back), but make sure that it fits snugly and gives good control; and yearlings, too, if they are well mannered. From then on, however, you should accustom the young horse to accepting a snaffle bit, so that you have a little more control in the ring. The unbroken three-year-old native pony may not be very big, but when excited can be very strong. Try to allow the young horse to meet as many different sights and sounds as possible, so that his first outing to a show is not too much of a surprise. If you accustom the youngster to other horses and handle him well, you should not have too many difficulties.

It is a good idea to teach the youngster to lead into a horsebox or trailer as part of his normal training so that when you come to show him this is not another new experience. Make it as pleasant as possible for the young pony: give him a reward in the shape of a small feed once he is in the trailer. Then he can be led out when your assistant has lowered the ramp. When the foal is walking confidently into the trailer or box, and appears unfussed, it is time to take him on a short journey.

One often hears grumbles at shows that pony classes are only for the people who can keep quality ponies stabled and can afford

Welsh Mountain ponies (Section A — the smallest type of Welsh pony). This pretty little mare and her foal show Arab breeding in their dark muzzle and eye markings, and the mare in her concave face and large gentle eyes. White grey is a typical colour of this breed.

the high prices they fetch today, but the child or small-time owner who cares for his own pony and keeps it at grass can have a lot of fun with a registered native pony which is likely to be a useful all-round family pony as well.

The advantage of a pedigree native pony is that you can show at all the big shows, many of which have both in-hand and ridden classes. The bigger breeds such as New Forest, Highland, Fell, or Welsh Cob can do well in family pony, riding or Pony Club events, as well as in their own breed classes. Many Welsh and Dartmoor ponies will also do well in show pony classes. In the native classes ponies should be shown in all their natural glory of flowing mane, tail and feather. This is the one difference, and causes many headaches when you want to show your long-maned native pony in an ordinary showing class where it needs a short mane for neat plaits! Native ponies are born to work and enjoy it, some even need regular work to remain tractable under saddle. They are ideal if you want to combine Pony Club and riding club events with showing, and they are excellent for long-distance riding.

Ridden classes

In the ridden mountain and moorland class the judge is looking for the best pony of its own breed. As in show pony classes, it must be well schooled, move well under saddle, and be capable of giving a nice show. Many mountain and moorland ponies are ideal for family pony classes, which have become more popular over the years, to give the useful all-rounder, who may not have the fineness and quality of the show pony, a chance in the ring. The family pony should nevertheless be good looking, well trained and good mannered; it does not have to be a pedigree. Any good cross-bred pony, nicely turned out and able to give a display without tricks (which so often spoils this class) is suitable, and this event also gives a chance to the pony and child who do not enjoy jumping. The pony will be similar in type to a working pony without so much quality, safe for a child to hunt or ride in Pony Club events, and of good sound conformation.

8 Children's riding ponies

Perhaps the most popular classes at horse shows today are for children's riding ponies. In England more quality ponies are bred than in any other country in the world, and if you are going to compete successfully you must have a quality pony as near perfect in conformation as possible, and really well trained. Most of these ponies are cross-bred from native breeds with Thoroughbred or Arab, as can be seen in the pony breeding classes where the breeders show their stock.

The pony should be compact (so that without a saddle you can see where the rider will sit) and be full of quality with a neat small head, and yet must still look like a pony and not a horse. Pony type is important as well as the temperament which, in the true pony type, is usually kind and generous.

Before you start showing, if you have not already done so you must register your pony with the British Show Pony Society. Members can gain help and advice from the area shows and evening discussions that are organised by the Society, and their handbook will give you full details and the rules of the classes. At all shows affiliated to the Society your pony must be registered in order to enter and must have an official height certificate, as all ponies are divided into height classes and can be ridden by children of certain ages according to the height of the pony. The principal classes are as follows:

Leading Rein Classes: pony not exceeding 12 hands to be ridden by a child up to 7 years old if the show is affiliated to the BSPS.

First Pony: all ponies must be 4 years old or over, not exceeding 12 hands and ridden off the leading rein by a child up to 9 years old.

Novice Pony: for a pony that has never won a first prize in cash valued £3 or over, up to and including the published closing date of entry, at shows affiliated to the BSPS. Ponies must wear snaffle bridles in novice classes.

Best Pony: not exceeding 12.2 hands to be ridden by a child 12 years and under.

Best Pony: exceeding 12.2 hands but not exceeding 13.2 hands to be ridden by a child 14 years and under.

Best Pony: exceeding 13.2 hands but not exceeding 14.2 hands to be ridden by a child 16 years and under.

The Working Pony classes, which have become very popular, also come under the British Show Pony Society Rules.

The leading rein class

For spectators, one of the favourite classes is the leading rein event. The judging of this class, and the first pony class which follows on, is different from show pony classes in that the judge is looking principally for perfect manners and a narrow, sensible steady pony that can be trusted with a small child under any circumstances; a fairly small, compact pony without extravagant action (which would throw a small child up too much at the trot) but rather a nice low, steady movement will help a small child to keep firm in the saddle. The pony must obviously be good looking, but however beautiful, if it does not seem suitable for a small child a good judge will not place it in this particular class. The Welsh ponies come into their own in leading rein classes, as being small and compact with beautiful little heads, they are ideal children's ponies. It is important for a pony to have a good head carriage as this helps the child to sit safely in the saddle. A pony with a tendency to a low head carriage is not good as it pulls a small child forward, especially if the child is inclined to be heavy on the hand.

The ideal leading rein pony should be a model toy pony, com-

Breeding and a sensible temperament show in the head of this riding pony, probably the result of careful cross-breeding of a native pony with a Thoroughbred, producing an extremely good-looking pony with a nice ride.

pact in body, able to stand square, move steadily with a nice head carriage, and be showy but gentle. It should in no way be strong, or thick through the wither, for a tiny child. On the other hand, a narrow miniature Thoroughbred type pony does not give the child enough to sit on safely as it must be remembered that young children rely mostly on balance, not grip. One judge may prefer a slightly bigger pony than a tiny one, feeling it gives a child more to sit on, while another may feel that a smaller, more compact pony is right for a young child.

Your pony must be neatly plaited, preferably with several small plaits rather than a few lumpy ones, and wear a nice show bridle, perhaps with a coloured browband. The saddle should be small enough for a child to ride on comfortably, and the web leading rein should be whitened. The condition and turnout of both rider and pony must be perfect to stand a chance at a big show.

Showing on the leading rein is an art, and as you are having to cope with the child as well as the pony, you will need to train the pony and child together at home, leading the two regularly before the show. Contrary to what many spectators think, only the pony is judged and not the child (unless at an unaffiliated show where there is a riding prize). However, it is no use having a good pony with a child that cannot ride nicely: the judge likes to see the pony stopped and turned by the rider, rather than by the leader, although the pony should be trained to obey the leader at all times. The leader must be sure to stay far enough away from the pony for the judge to see it! A judge will not penalize an old pony unless this affects its appearance or movement, as in this class safety of the child is all-important.

The procedure for the leading rein class is as follows: First the ponies are led round the ring for the judge to see them. It is important to give yourself room and keep a nice long length of lead rein, but be ready to check the pony if needed. You will then wait your turn to trot past the judge one at a time. If you are lucky enough to be picked for the front row you will be asked to give an individual show. Remember to remain unhurried and to keep your distance from the pony, so that the judge can clearly see his good points.

First pony class

The first pony class is the natural follow-on from the leading rein class, designed to start the child off the leading rein in the show

Opposite top Divide the mane into even sections, fastened with elastic bands, before starting to braid.

Opposite below Braid each hank of hair, binding the end tightly with cotton and leaving the ends of the cotton free.

Overleaf top Thread the loose ends of cotton through a blunt darning needle, roll up the braids, turning the ends under and sew them up.

Overleaf below Neat braids give your horse a smart appearance for the ring.

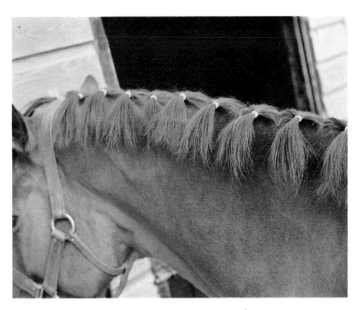

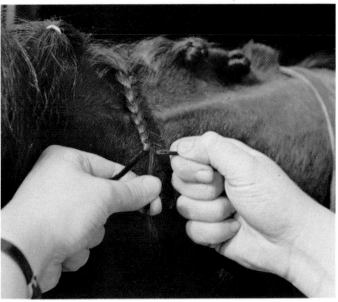

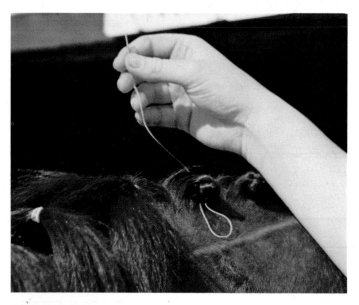

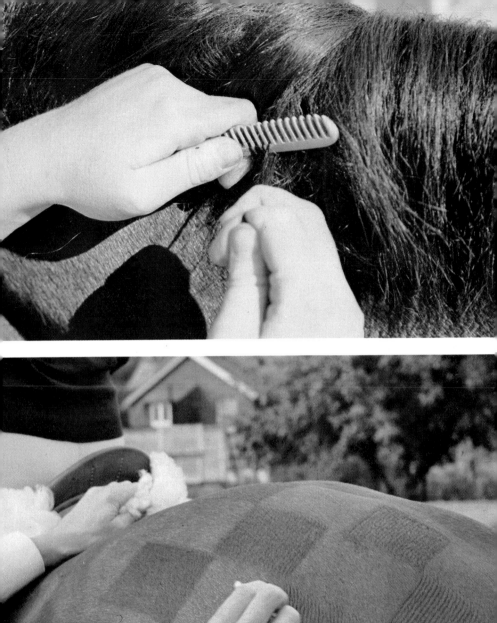
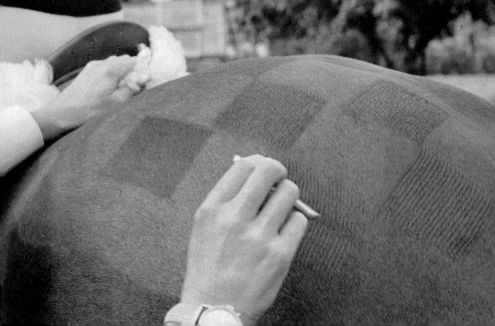

ring. It is a rule of this class that children should only trot when going round the ring together. As the age limit is nine years and under, and most children are just off the leading rein, this is a wise rule so that the children do not lose confidence should the ponies start galloping or get out of hand. The ponies are judged at the walk and trot and then lined up. When there is time, or at a smaller show, the judge will allow all the children to give an individual display. The child may be asked to canter so that the judge can see how the pony goes for a small child at a faster pace, and he will also notice how kindly it obeys the child in going away from the other ponies. Manners are most important in this class, more so than in the leading rein class, as the pony must be a real school-master to take care of the child at all times. The child must be able to show the pony in hand, as this class is also judged on conformation.

Very often, the same pony can win both leading rein and first pony classes. The main difference is that the first pony is more of a safe pet pony for a child, than the smarter, showy lead rein pony. Spectators will often see the same ponies in the line-up, but perhaps in a different order as there will be a different rider on top and no leader, and also because in the first pony class the judge is looking for a pony and child that go happily and safely together on their own.

In all other ridden pony classes, ponies must be four-years-old, but in the novice class, they can be shown as three-year-olds after 1 July. However, you must be careful not to overdo the schooling and showing as young ponies, like young children, quickly become bored; four or five shows are plenty for a three-year-old in the first season.

Previous page (top) Pulling the horse's mane to thin and shorten it is best done by twisting hair around a mane comb.

Previous page (below) Decorative patterns on the horse's quarters can be made with the help of a mane comb.

Opposite To clean the saddle, remove dirt with a well squeezed out sponge and warm water then apply saddle soap with a nearly-dry sponge.

Show pony classes

The 'Best Pony' or show pony classes are of great importance to breeders, because they prove whether or not a stud is breeding on the right lines, and a pony stallion siring a champion pony can be the making of a stud. Breeders follow the winning ponies' pedigrees very closely, and it is interesting to see how many of the winners are bred by the same breeders, or by the same pony stallion. This is one aspect which parents of young competitors often do not realize, as they are looking at it from a different angle. The pony breeder is anxious to breed the most beautiful pony, and conformation is of prior importance, while the parent is more interested in a pony that will give a polished performance. This is where the judge is often criticized (the poor judge is never considered right except by the winner!). It is the judge's job to weigh up the best combination of conformation, performance and manners in one pony to find the winner.

The three show pony classes vary little in their requirements. In the 12.2 hands class riders go on a bit faster in their show to do an extended canter, and in the two larger divisions the ponies are expected to gallop on singly. In fact, a pony that can really stretch over the ground in long strides at the gallop is at a great advantage when it comes to the final judging for a championship. There is a slight difference of type in each class. They must all be quality ponies, but the 12.2 hands ponies must be very much of pony type that is, small and compact, full of pony character and suitable for a small child. Quality must prevail, but you would not want such a fine blood pony (unless perfectly mannered) for a young child in this class as in the two bigger classes.

In the 13.2 hands and 14.2 hands pony classes, riders are up to fourteen and sixteen years of age respectively, so you get some very competent riders who are more than capable of riding a keen blood pony. In my opinion, all well-schooled ponies should be well-mannered and there is no excuse for the finely bred pony not behaving as impeccably as any other.

The 14.2 hands class is where one has to look for pony type, as sometimes one finds a pony that gives the impression of being a small horse or hack type rather than a pony. The judge will be looking for pony type, combined with quality and that elusive element, presence.

In all three divisions the riders are expected to show their ponies round the ring at walk, trot and canter, with a single change of rein. Then, after lining up, some will be selected to give a short show. For the single display, the pony and rider should walk away from the line, give a nice extended trot (not too fast!), a figure-of-eight at the canter and, if required, a gallop on, followed by a rein back and halt in front of the judge. The final judging of conformation then takes place, the ponies being unsaddled, led up to the judge for inspection, and trotted past him in hand. This gives him a chance to look for good and bad points and blemishes, to check for soundness, good straight movement and that there are no signs of unevenness of stride, throwing of feet, or other faults. Finally the ponies are saddled up again and walked round while the judge puts together all he has seen and selects the winners. There may well be a change round from the original line-up: if a pony has not given a good display it will be moved down; on closer examination, a pony down the line may have been found to have beautiful limbs and conformation and will come up. The child and pony should be at their best until the rosettes are given, for the class may not be completely decided until just before the awards are announced!

Working pony classes

One of the most successful innovations at shows in recent years has been the working pony class, which has become very popular. The original idea came from America, where there is a strong pony hunter division in which the ponies are judged on their performance over fences, not just as show models of ponies. The idea caught on in England and there are now four classes for working ponies organized by the BSPS.

Nursery Stakes: for ponies not exceeding 13 hands, for riders of 11 years and under. Fences minimum 2ft (61cm), maximum 2ft 3in (68.6cm).

Ponies not exceeding 13 hands: for riders 14 years and under. Fences minimum 2ft 6in (76.2cm), maximum 3ft (91.5cm).

Ponies exceeding 13 hands but not exceeding 14 hands: for riders 16 years and under. Fences minimum 2ft 9in (83.9cm), maximum 3ft. 3in (97.8cm).

Ponies exceeding 14 hands but not exceeding 15 hands: for riders 18 years and under. Fences minimum 3ft (91.5cm), maximum 3ft 6in (106.7cm).

The winners of these classes at qualifying shows go on to compete at the Working Pony Championships at Peterborough in September. These championships have become the supreme award for working ponies, and the highlight of the show season for the many families involved in showing working ponies.

A working pony should be similar in type to the working hunter, but of pony type. Ideally it should have quality but with more bone than one would require in a show pony, and with the substance to do a day's hunting: it needs to be both workmanlike and handsome. This class is judged on an entirely different system from that of the show pony classes. There are two phases, with marks added up to find the winner. These marks are awarded as follows:

Phase One:	Jumping	50
	Style and manners while jumping	10
Phase Two:	Conformation and freedom of action	30
	Manners	10
	Total	100

Penalties:

Phase One:	Jumping knock down	10
	First refusal	15
	Second refusal	20
	Third refusal	Elimination
	Fall of horse or rider	20
	(A complete turn round consitutes a refusal)	

The judging is very similar to that for the working hunter horse jumping phase, but with more emphasis on manners. Marks are awarded for style and for each jump, and at most shows the standard is so high that only clear rounds stand any chance of reaching the final judging. The course consists of a series of hunting-type natural fences with at least one change of direction, that each competitor jumps in turn. The pony is not required to be a show jumper, but the type of safe, sure-footed jumper that is suitable for the hunting field. His schooling must include plenty of practice over a variety of natural obstacles, and he should be ridden at a good hunting pace without stopping and starting, but kept firmly under the rider's control in case an emergency stop should be necessary. After the jumping phase the ponies come back into the ring together and are called in line in order of their jumping marks. Next they come out singly to give a show which should include a gallop, after which the pony should pull up well and come to a halt. This gives the judge a chance to assess the pony's movement, manners and training. Finally, conformation is scrutinized as in any other class, with the judge looking for sound, clean limbs, good feet, a good shoulder, a well put on head, strong quarters with a good second thigh, a compact pony build, a nice outlook with presence, and good straight action. It will be noticed that the height requirements in the three divisions for working ponies are slightly different from those in the show pony classes; this gives ponies that do not measure for show classes another chance, enabling the slightly larger, more sturdily built, quality ponies to compete in the show ring.

9 The Arab

The Ridden Events Committee of the Arab Horse Society has a slogan, 'If you ride, ride an Arab', although in fact Arab enthusiasts have had to overcome considerable bias from followers of other types. Until recently a great many misguided people thought the mere fact that they owned a pure-bred Arabian was sufficient qualification to appear in the show ring, regardless of whether or not it was a good show specimen. Happily things are now changing: Arab owners are becoming educated both from the point of view of riding and producing a better class of animal, and of tak-

A Russian-bred Arab stallion, with a beautiful, classical concave face and large dark eyes. His long quarter and high tail carriage make him very elegant. He is the embodiment of his romantic ancestry, and can easily be imagined galloping over the deserts of Arabia, fleet and sure-footed.

An Anglo-Arab superbly turned out for the show ring; his long tail neatly
'banged' and plaited, his mane, also plaited, shows his elegant neck. His
coat shines and his neat hoofs are oiled to make a perfect turnout.

ing much more care about the correct schooling and presentation
of it. The judges, too, are more aware of the basic needs of the
ridden Arab and there is less tendency to put up the one with the
best conformation over the better schooled, but perhaps plainer,
animal. The part-breds and Anglos, who also come under the
auspices of the Arab Horse Society, have tended to be better off
as they are often judged by the same judges as hack and hunter
classes, which has brought with it a much higher standard in their
production; in fact, a great many Anglo and part-bred Arabs have
been top class show horses and big winners.

Breeders who have the welfare and future of the Arabian at
heart are encouraging people to geld all but the very best colts.
Arab blood has, over a long period of time, been infused to improve many other breeds. One would do well to remember that
many Thoroughbreds trace back to the Byerley Turk, the
Goldolphin Arabian and the Darley Arabian. The genuine desert
Arabian was exceptionally hardy, fleet of foot, and possessed
enormous stamina. Today's Arabian is a graceful and co-ordinated
creature, unusually alert and quick on its feet, and compact in
build. The back is short with a fairly level croup and high-set tail,
the head, upon an elegant neck, is dish-faced and delicate, with

87

large, wide-set eyes and flaring nostrils in a tiny muzzle; the ears are intelligent and point towards each other. An average horse is fairly small, usually standing between 14.1 and 15.1 hands.

Arab show classes

At a small show you are likely to be able to compete in one ridden class — 'For pure-bred, Anglo - and part-bred Arabs, stallions, mares and geldings, four years old and upwards, to be ridden and judged as riding horses'. However, the bigger the show the greater your choice. At a county show one would expect to find the pure-breds divided from the part-breds and Anglo-Arabs, while some newer shows being run by the various regions of the Arab Horse Society are divided still further: two classes for pure-breds, one for stallions and one for mares and geldings. Part-breds and Anglo-Arabs may also be separated, and could be split still further with a height division of either 14.2 or 15 hands.

A pure-bred mare or gelding will never have the presence of a stallion, and will therefore have to go exceptionally well to be at one — an obvious disadvantage in mixed classes. The Arab Horse Society has recognized this, and to encourage owners it gives special awards to the highest-placed mare or gelding in a mixed class. Small horses also may be at a disadvantage, as it is usual for the judge to ride the horses, and a tall judge is unlikely to have a comfortable ride on a very small mount.

To produce your Arab correctly for the show ring takes a great deal of time and patience in order to school him thoroughly in the basic principles that are expected of all horses. He must go forward with impulsion and enthusiasm under control, with correct rhythm in all his paces, and he must also have the correct bend. All these things he must learn to do in a snaffle bridle before you ever consider putting on a double or a pelham.

The trot is the Arab's outstanding gait, but before you can ask for true extension you must have established a really good working trot. This is very important, since many otherwise good horses tend either to be high behind or have bad hocks. With correct schooling these weaknesses can be improved. Horses that are trotting as fast as they can lay their legs to the ground, with their noses stuck in the air and their hocks flying out behind them, may look spectacular to the uninitiated but they are actually out of rhythm and lacking balance, making for nasty unlevel paces and a jarring, unbalanced ride. It is, therefore, important to work your horse on both reins and to rise to the trot equally on both diagonals. This will help the horse to become supple and give a balanced ride. He must also become accustomed to being ridden by more than one rider, so that he will be prepared to give the judge a well-mannered ride in the show ring.

The requirements in most ridden Arab classes are that you walk, trot, canter (sometimes changing the rein in canter) and gallop on. Occasionally you will be asked to give an individual show: trot canter on both reins, gallop on, stop, stand still and rein back. The rider's turnout at a small show could be a tweed jacket, collar and tie, jodhpurs and hat, but at the larger shows a black or navy-blue coat would be more correct. Your horse can wear a snaffle bridle at a small show, but he must be shown in a double once county standard is reached. Remember that careful training, preparation, good presentation and riding are a winning combination.

An Arab stallion; essentially a small breed, but capable of carrying a lot of weight. Strong, hardy and sound, the Arab is perhaps the most beautiful breed, and one which has influenced the majority of breeds.

10 Side-saddle

Nowhere at a show is there a more elegant and graceful sight than the side-saddle class, which is growing enormously in popularity.

Before entering for a side-saddle class yourself it will be well worth while to go to an expert for advice and a few lessons first. Ideally the horse you learn on should already be accustomed to being ridden side-saddle. You will probably want to ride side-saddle for the very reason that it does look so beautiful, so you want to do it correctly. Riding side-saddle is not, in fact, at all difficult — but it will feel a bit different the first time you try! You always have to be given a leg-up into the saddle so remember, in the show ring, to have some one suitable on hand. He will be needed after your horse has been individually led out in hand for the judge.

A side-saddle is designed to be ridden on the left side and it has two pommels, over one of which the rider rests her right leg, placing the left leg under the lower pommel. The seat is often made of doeskin. It is essential to have a saddle that fits your mount properly; on some ponies a balance strap is helpful to prevent slipping. Older saddles have out-of-date safety fittings and it may be impossible to find suitable stirrup leather fittings.

Once in the saddle, you will find that you are really only sitting on your right buttock! What is more, you will convey most of the aids with your seat, so it is essential to have a well-schooled horse. There will be no leg aids on the right-hand side, although a tap with a long stick may be given if necessary.

The first thing to remember is to keep your right shoulder well back because this keeps you straight in the saddle. Your hands should be held low and not, as is all too often seen, clutching the reins above the wither as if hanging on to a bunch of knitting! Add to the grace by sitting upright with a nice straight back, tummy muscles in, but do not stiffen — relax yourself, and your

Riding a show hunter at the Richmond Royal Horse Show, wearing a silk hat, veil, stock, well-fitting dark jacket and skirt, and light gloves. The saddle and double bridle are impeccable, with all the metal gleaming.

horse will not tense up either. It is surprising how secure you will feel, no matter what mischief your horse gets up to, so long as you remember to keep that right shoulder back. Do not attempt to rise at the trot, as a sitting trot is used in side-saddle riding; you will be even more comfortable at the canter, flowing over the ground in complete unison with your horse.

Ladies' hack class

The side-saddle ladies' hack class often brings a change of form from astride classes, as a larger hack with a longer back and low stride has a tendency to give a more comfortable side-saddle ride than a more compact little horse. The class is judged as in other hack classes but, besides the ride side-saddle, the judge is looking for the hack that goes smoothly and easily for the rider. This requires a higher standard of training than with astride riding and here the older, more experienced hack has the advantage over the younger horse. You need to be able to convey to the horse with the slightest movement what you want him to do, and this can be practised astride at home until perfected.

Pony classes

Pony side-saddle classes are also judged on the pony, although some classes have been introduced where it is the best side-saddle rider that is looked for. This seems a good idea to further the standard of riding.

Turnout

The habit for riding side-saddle should be a plain navy blue with the apron (skirt) of heavy material so that it hangs straight and does not billow in the wind. In the final judging of the major shows a silk hat and veil and stock are worn, while a bowler hat and tie are more usual for the preliminary stages. Gloves are worn by both ladies and children. Spurs are not allowed in pony classes.

Two judges inspect a hack for conformation, at the Royal Windsor Horse Show. Any skimping over cleaning the saddle will be evident at this stage. The horse is well turned-out, with decorative 'quartering' on his rump. His rider wears the less formal bowler and tie, quite correct together.

11 Driving at shows

Driving at shows can be a very rewarding experience, particularly when it is realized just how much the watching public appreciates the old-world sight of horses and ponies in harness.

Travelling

The first item to be considered is how best to travel, for there are several methods. Some people prefer boxing their horse, or horses, in a low-load trailer with the carriage mounted on the towing vehicle. The advantage of this is that everything except the horse can be loaded well in advance. Another method is for both carriage and animals to be carried on separate low-load trailers, but this requires two towing vehicles. A third type of transport can be achieved with a motor horsebox large enough to carry the entire turnout, vehicle and its horse or horses. In bad weather this is ideal, but it is essential to ensure that in an emergency the horse can be unloaded quickly and easily. Apart from the transport of carriage and horse, the harness requires careful packing in containers.

Preparation

In order to succeed at shows today an extremely high standard must be achieved, so the vehicle and harness should be both painted and polished to maximum effect. The actual colouring of the vehicle should be thought out in advance to complement the horse. Most colour combinations suit blacks, greys, bays, and browns, while palominos and bright chestnuts are not enhanced by either scarlet or bright yellow near them. On the whole, carriage colours should be subdued or dark and never garish. In some cases, however, duns and palominos in particular can look very arresting when harnessed to a vehicle of an almost exactly matching colour — varnished woodwork, for instance — although this style is used in rustic vehicles only, such as floats, governess carts, dog carts or wagonettes. In addition to suiting the colour of the vehicle to the horse, the actual types of both should be considered. Stocky ponies, such as Dales, Fells, Welsh Cobs, Shetlands and Exmoors, need sporty or rustic vehicles, while animals with finer limbs (Hackneys, or cross-bred horses and ponies with Arab or Thoroughbred blood) require the more elegant phaetons and gigs. Harnesses, too, should be of the correct type for the turnout, rustic vehicles requiring either brown or black leather, while patent leather should be reserved for the smarter vehicles.

In addition to the appearance of the horse, which of course must be well-groomed, with its hooves oiled and its mane appropriately taken care of (either brushed out or plaited), the outfit of the driver and his attendant groom (who is essential for safety's sake) must also be considered. Elegance, not flashiness, is the goal. Fancy dress or period costume should never be worn except when appearing in displays or pageants. An apron and gloves should be worn by both sexes. The whip must be carried at all times in order to urge on, correct, or possibly to distract the horse in an emergency.

Before the start of a class, a short session of 'warming-up', walking and trotting about the grounds, makes good sense as it will help to calm an over-exuberant horse and also loosen any stiff joints.

At the show

It is customary to be lined up for inspection before going out either to do an individual 'show' around the ring, or for the drive on the road. The judge will examine harness for its cleanliness, suppleness, and fit. Vehicles are looked at not only for their appearance but also for their size and suitability for the horse. The horse itself is judged firstly on conformation — its most important attributes being depth of heart and the possession of a 'leg at each

A prize-winning Hackney pony, with typical action, driven to a show wagon.

corner' ending in good feet which are well shod. Its action, which need not be exaggerated but should be free and flowing, is noted, but above all its manners are important, so that even with courage and presence it is both obedient and suitable for an amateur to drive. Judges also often ask to see what spares are carried, as these are important when going out on the road.

In the road section, judges usually try to conceal themselves at strategic points so that, unseen, they can gain a better idea of the horses' performances than in the ring. Then, on their return, they examine them for fitness — excessive sweating, for example will lose marks.

Back in the ring again, the atmosphere becomes really tense when driving round for the final selection. It is now that drivers should proceed with extra caution, for it must be remembered that other competitors may be having problems to cope with, trying to hold back an over-keen horse or perhaps to push on a reluctant one. In all cases, it is wise to steer very clear of other turnouts. Rushing past too closely is more than likely to cause an upset of some sort. It is best to hold well back, even to slow down at corners, in order to give your horse a clear run down the side of the ring.

After the class has finished, do not remove the bridle until the horse is free from the vehicle. This is potentially extremely dangerous and many accidents have been caused this way. The proper procedure is always first to undo the breeching straps, then to remove the traces, unbuckle the belly band, and then, with an assistant, lead the horse away from the vehicle. Only then can his bridle be replaced by a headcollar with safety.

Show classes

Classes may be divided into sections for singles and pairs and tandems of different heights, as well as into non-Hackney and Hackney types.

Scurry driving — the 'show jumping' of driving — is a recent but popular innovation in the show ring. Classes are open to both singles and pairs and the vehicle has to pass through a series of obstacles at speed, the winners being judged purely on performance.

Perhaps the most interesting driving competitions of all are the three-day events of combined driving, with three consecutive days of various driving manoeuvres — a dressage drive, endurance drive, and an obstacle course with turns and figures to be executed — to decide the final victor.